AF604834

There are many different groups of First Australians. Different groups may speak different languages.

There were more than 250 languages. Now there are only around 120. Most of these could soon be lost.

This is the Pinkenba War Memorial. Pinkenba is a suburb in Brisbane. Its name comes from the Turrbal word binkinba. Binkinba means “place of land tortoise”.

Porongurup is a small town in Western Australia. Its name comes from the Noongar word purrengorep. Purrengorep means “meeting place near water”.

PORONGURUP
VILLAGE
20 km
252

This is a photo of Amaroo and Ngunnawal. They are two suburbs of Canberra. Amaroo means “a beautiful place”.

The First Peoples were sometimes told to stop using their languages. They did not learn their own language.

The Purnululu National Park is in Western Australia. Purnululu comes from the Djaru word Bullmanlulu. This is the name of an area near the Bungle Bungle mountains.

PURNULULU
NATIONAL PARK
53
Növak
(BUNGLE BUNGLE)

Goolwa is a town in South Australia. Goolwa means “elbow”.

In an emergency
dial 000
Goolwa Beach
WARNING
Rough Surf
Strong Currents
Snakes
INFORMATION

Croajingolong National Park is in Victoria. Croajingolong comes from two Krauatungalung words. Galung means “belonging to”. Kraua means “east”.

C617
Gipsy Point
Mallacoota
Croajingolong Nat. Pk
Genoa
GENERAL STORE

Nitmiluk National Park is in the Northern Territory. Nitmiluk means “place of the cicada Dreaming”.

Nitmiluk National Park
Leliyn (Edith Falls) 20

This is a photo of the Great Lake. Great Lake is near Liawanee in Tasmania. Liawanee means “cold”. Tasmania can be very cold!

Word bank

beautiful

cicada

different

languages

meeting

memorial

mountains

photo

suburb

tortoise

By Mayvel Datuin

Edited by Marizel Cabigting
Arranged and designed by Tess Ritumalta

ISBN:
Hardbound-978-621-470-184-1
Mobile/Kindle-978-621-470-185-8
Softbound/Paperback- 978-621-470-186-5

Published in the Philippines by:
Poetry Planet Book Publishing House
Rosario, Pozorrubio, Pangasinan, Philippines
Contact No.: 09554960044
Email: maritesritumalta@gmail.com

JOURNEY WITH UNEXPECTED PROPOSAL

Written by

Mayvel Datuin

INTRODUCTION

Great day to all readers let me introduce myself: My name is Mayvel Datuin, Certified Pharmacy Technician (CPhT). Founder of Aakf PH Community Event, "We Create Smile". I am married for 14 years and I have one adorable little boy, and his name is Erik. I am a Filipino currently living in California. I love to learn things outside my comfort zone, listen to music, travel with my family, and taste different kinds of food. I was Born in Mulanay Quezon Province Philippines, and raised in Lapaz, Leyte Philippines.

SYNOPSIS

The Journey with Unexpected Proposal is a story of a woman who believes in herself and of the saying, “Sky is the limit”. She shares her journey from her childhood days up to her married life revealing various emotions of happiness, sadness, excitements, struggles, longings, faith, determination, courage, and success. Life is beautiful and full of unexpected surprises. There are moments when we must decide quickly and then follow our instinct in whatever choices we chose in life.

"Life is a journey with problems to solve and lessons to learn but most of all, Experiences to enjoy." *Unknown*

TABLE OF CONTENTS

PART 1

WHO I AM

I was born in Mulanay, Quezon Province, Philippines, and raised in Lapaz, Leyte, Philippines. I have two younger brothers and one elder sister. In the compound surrounded by my aunts, our happy family raised us. Since my parents have their own work, they were able to provide us with our needs. My mother bought and sold RTW, while my father worked in a big tailoring company somewhere in Batangas. My father's job required him to live near the location of his work so he would come home every weekend only. Generally, my mother and my aunts took the responsibility of taking care of us, children. Sometimes, my mother and father argued. It is but normal for couples to argue and for many reasons. However, my parent's issue was fidelity. My siblings and I were very young then and we do not understand it that much. We felt hurt seeing them argue and become indifferent to each other.

One night, my mother and I were running after my father in the middle of the street. My mother was crying, and so was I, while my father slowly disappeared from our sight. Just like a glass that dropped and then shattered, my beautiful and happy family was gone.

They tried to fix it but it still ended in separation. My mother decided to bring us, children, to Leyte where her parents live. But when it comes to the whereabouts of my father, we never have any hint of a clue either. I was only six years old at the time my parents separated.

As I was growing up, I remembered how I respond when a relative or a friend asked me, “Hey! May, what do you want to be when you grow up?” I just looked at them for a moment and answered, “I am not sure yet, but for sure I want to get an education; It was always like that.”

When I saw a young girl carrying her own baby, I always tell myself, “Hey, May, you will never become like that!” That was because I always envision myself doing better and so I kept focusing on my dream. I also had ambition and goals in life. I actually wrote them on my imaginary white paper. This paper had my lists no one else knew except me. They were the lists I wanted to have and become in my life. I had a short-term plan and a long-term plan. WHY? Because If I failed my long-term plan, I would at least have my back-ups, which were my short-term plans. On my list the first one is to have an education, the second was to acquire a stable job. The third was of helping my siblings/family. My fourth goal is to travel around the world. The fifth was to find my true love with the one who will accept me the way I am. My sixth list included getting married

when I turned 25 years old. Seventh on the list was to own a house, my very own dream house. The eighth goal was to have a child, while my ninth was to share my blessings with others, and many more. To make sure that all on my lists would happen I made a concession, that I will not pressure myself and that all I have to do is to focus on my education and on getting a job. I knew it would come true one day. Only God knows when the right time is.

PART 2

COURAGE

Our life in my grandparents' house was so different from what we had when we were still with my parents. We were already trained at a young age to learn to do house chores like washing the dishes, cleaning the house, folding our clothes, etc. During weekends, we helped Uncle June wash clothes for our neighbors, family friends, or anyone else in the community. It was a great struggle back then, and there were many cases when I went to school without breakfast. My grandmother would give me money for recess as long as she had coins, that too happens rarely. We were lucky if we could eat meals three times a day and it was a bonus if we could even have some snacks. Though it was very challenging, we never complained. My siblings and I were still very lucky that we have our grandparents, uncles, and aunties who loved us and guided us. Even though we do not have enough money, a nice house, or many other things most kids have, we still feel blessed and contented. I always looked at the bright side. In addition, my hopes are high, fully believing that one day my life would change. I cannot be poor forever.

I remind myself that I had to focus on my studies, and if could, I would get an extra job, to be able to support my school expenses and of course, I also wanted to provide for my siblings. At my young age, you could say I was already mature. You would never see me playing or roaming and fooling around with friends. I chose to be productive. After I went to school, I would drop by Mrs. Pulma's house to do errands like watering her plants and going to the market to buy what they needed. She would then give me money and feed me before I went home. On my way back home, I would buy some bread for me, and my siblings.

During summer, I worked as a saleslady in my relative's grocery store or helped my teacher clean their house, yards, or do anything they asked me to. I would receive wages that I used in purchasing the school supplies I needed for the upcoming school year. These became my regular routines until I finished high school. Thanks to all my relatives, my mentors who guided and helped me, and who was always reminding me that I finish my education.

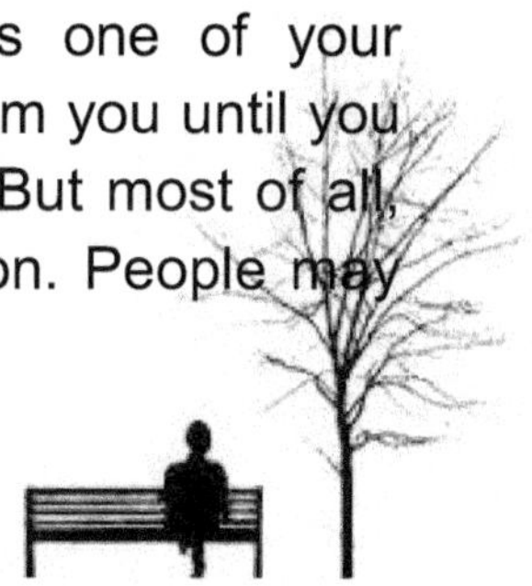

I could still remember so well what Mrs. Esperanza Pulma, one of my Angel, who is now in heaven, told me, "Mayvel study hard. Education is one of your weapons that nobody can take away from you until you die. Education will take you anywhere. But most of all, take care of yourself and your reputation. People may not remember you nor your name, but what you did will always leave a lasting mark."

"Courage is the most important of all virtues because, without courage, you cannot practice any other virtue."

Family
Like
branches on a
tree we all grow
in different
directions,
but our
roots
keep
us all
together

PART 3

MOMENTS AND MEMORIES

During the year 2000, I finished High School. Some of my friends were preparing for college, but as for me, I could not go to college. One month later after my graduation, one of my grandmothers' sisters named Lola Rosa asked if I wanted to work, I told her I would. She asked if I wanted to work at her daughter's house. I said yes, I would. On our way to our destination which was in Samar, we visited one of my aunt's sister-in-law in Tacloban. Exactly during that time, she was looking for a nanny. I ended up working with her sister-in-law instead. It turned out to be a good deal for me because Mr. and Mrs. Monge was a very kind and very loving couple. They had three children, one girl, and two boys and they were the guardians of two more little boys. I felt safe and loved by this family. I remembered that they offered me to go to college free of charge, but I declined. I stayed with them for a couple of years. Later on, I needed to go, but I took with me lessons from them like how to pray the rosary, and how to develop and keep self-discipline. They also warned that during mealtimes, we should never spill our food on the table or the floor. If we did, we would have to pick it up ourselves and eat it. Every six o'clock before dinner, we

had to pray the rosary. Well, I learned so many positive and beautiful things from them, which had become very useful to me, and my little boy. Nevertheless, I had to say goodbye to them not because I was not happy with them, but because I was kind of “soul-searching”. I would really like to find my long-lost father. I even set aside the idea of going to college even if I really wanted to.

Thank you ate Adel, Kuya Cesar, and the kids for guiding me and showing me warm love and affection. You had proven that a happy family still exists. I was very lucky and blessed, and I would always cherish those wonderful memories with all of you.

“The most beautiful things are not associated with money; they are memories and moments.” *Unknown*

At
18
sparkle
and shine...
...like the star
you are!

PART 4

MY 18TH BIRTHDAY

By the Year 2001, I turned 18, this was the first time I again celebrated my birthday since my parents separated. I do not want to celebrate my birthday but my mother and stepfather insisted on giving me a simple birthday celebration. On my 18th birthday, it was raining hard then it continued to be a typhoon of signal #1, only during that day. Then the following day it looked like no typhoon happened yesterday. My mom told me that the typhoon might be my twin. Hehehehe. I thanked my mother and stepfather for their gift, it was so unforgettable and it meant a lot to me.

By the year 2002, my eldest sister was already in Manila. She soon met my father. In time, I was to go there, too, once she finishes her course. While waiting for my turn to go to college, I searched for a job again. My mother finds me one in a Pharmacy. I worked for a couple of years there. My boss was awesome, she owned the pharmacy and even taught me how to be a pharmacy technician. I loved working there; I also met new friends and co-workers. Again, the time has come for me to say goodbye to my boss and my co-workers.

The experiences I had equipped me with more confidence making me well prepared to face a new journey.

"Never regret. If it's good, it's wonderful. If it's bad, it's experience." - *Victoria Holt*

PART 5

FORGIVENESS

By the year 2003, I met my dear father. We had not seen each other for a very long time. I kept asking myself, “Where have you been for 14 years?” The search was finally over this time. It was surreal to see him for more than a decade. I felt that the gap in my heart created by our separation had once again reconnected. We learned to forgive him and my mother for all they had done to us. We moved on and continued to live in the present. Then after a year, my youngest brother also came to Manila. I was thankful and blessed for learning to forgive my parents because it healed our aching hearts and it brought back happiness to all of us. The truth is, life must go on and it would be better to start new memories.

"Holding a grudge doesn’t make you strong; it makes you bitter. Forgiving doesn’t make you weak; it sets you free." – *Realistic Buddhism*

My sister finished her Office Technology Program. It was my turn to go to college. I took the same Program my sister took because, during those times, the University of Makati does not have Pharmacy Program.

While I was taking my classes, I met classmates with whom I became friends. We enjoyed each other's company. We loved being singles and we giggled together as we watch and observe our crushes on the campus. We enjoyed sitting and eating our snacks at our favorite spot at Makati Park after classes. It was fun. Sometimes some groups of girls attacked us because their crushes tagged along with us. Hahaha! It was fun.

Summer is coming, so I planned to get a summer job. My sister and I applied to work for one of the biggest companies in the Philippines called Bench and Human Company. Yes, I was hired! You might think it was that easy to get a job in Manila, but it was not. Wow! There were so many applicants for a couple of work vacancies. I was praying and hoping that they would choose me and hear them call my name. Waiting for the result almost took one full day. The human resource person came out at last; she had with her lists of names that were hired. "Oh, Lord!" My heart almost skipped a beat when my name was called, I was really surprised! "Yeppieeee! I got hired!" From then on, I spent my summer working for the Bench Company as their cashier.

After summer, I had to resume my classes. There were some subjects I needed to take up. Then, I would be done with my program after this semester. Yet, I do not

want to quit my job, so I spoke with my manager regarding my schooling.

PART 6

REWARD

By the year 2005, when my last semester was about to end, my On The Job Training at an Office was to come next. However, while I was still taking up the rest of my subjects, I continued working for the Bench Company. Since my manager allowed me to work when I do not have my classes, everything turned out well for me. During my school hours, she would assign me to a closing schedule and during my off days, I would work the daytime schedules. I learned to balance my time for work and school skillfully. It was so toxic in Manila. The city was bustling with busy people and it was common to be jammed in unending traffic. It was quite a struggle and challenge to juggle your schedules only to be present in your classes and work on time. I had to wake up early then went back home late or much later. Yet, I felt rewarded and relieved once my grades show soaring scores, not to mention receiving nice paychecks every two weeks. Oh yeah, these were my routine until I graduated from my Office Technology Program.

"The highest reward for a person's toil is not what they get for it, but what they become by it." *John Ruskin*

My Certificate

By the year 2005, I finished my contract with Bench/Human Company. They offered me another contract for their company but I declined this time because I had to start training in an Office. It was at the Don Bosco Technical College Mandaluyong. It was a school originally intended for boys exclusively. My training assignment was at the ISTC department. My duty description was a receptionist. I also had to look after all of the computer laboratories and made sure they were ready for use during classes. Aside from working that, I also learned how to use those computers, from writing e-mails to browsing social media.

In April 2005, I finished my program then after that, I got a job offer from my boss. I no longer had to search for a job myself. I guess my hard work paid off.

"The moment you give your best in whatever you do in life, it is easy to reach your goal. Always pray to God and believe in yourself that you can do it. Keep exploring and learn more." *Unknown*

PART 7

PROMOTION

Then the year 2006 arrived. This year, I received a promotion to a position. It was almost 2 years already from the time I started working for this company. I really enjoyed working at ISTC with some of my friends, the Bosses, and Students Assistants. We also enjoyed Annual office retreats to some beautiful resorts somewhere in Batangas and Laguna.

I realized that living my own life independently was awesome and I lived my life back then to the full. Paydays were always the best and we always made sure that we girls had our night out. We would go out for dinner to a live music restaurant, dance over the dance floor, meet new people and just chill out. Our rental house was a walking distance at our workplace which is why we do not need to rush to avoid traffic as most people do. The landlady though was very strict and would never allow boys to be our guests. However, we had our ate Menchie to thank for since she helped me and my friends had so much fun even though we really are silly sometimes. Hahahaha! I love those memories with Aj, Nove, Cecile, and Ann Hehehehe.

Most of us are now married and have our own kids, but as for Aj, she is still single and is ready to mingle.

My Big Decision

Late in January 2007, I received a message from my aunt who worked in Brunei. She asked me if I wanted to work abroad. I was undecided whether to accept the offer because I was already satisfied with my job. It also pays well. However, one of my dreams was to travel abroad. After giving much thought to it, I finally decided to accept it. I probably just followed my instinct. The truth is I never expected this to eventually materialize, but with this new adventure ahead, I had to make sure to prepare myself so well. I do not have any experience in this part, but I still believe I can do it. If someone can do it, so can I. That was how determined I was back then.

"A strong woman knows she has strength enough for the journey, but a woman of strength knows it is in the journey where she will become strong." *Unknown*

PART 8

MY FIRST TRIP

Looking back by the year 2007, my papers and plane ticket for traveling abroad were already in process. It was hard for me to resign from my work. Therefore, I just told my boss that I would only go for a vacation. However, the truth was, I was not planning to come back anymore. In February 2007, I left the Philippines. My first stop was in Malaysia, the agent picked me up at the airport then we slept at the hotel. Early the next morning, our travel agent along with some people rode by car and traveled for Brunei by Land. It was my very first international long journey after which we traveled by boat. After a couple of hours, a beautiful mosque in gold mesmerized my sight and I thought that we might already be in Brunei. Yes indeed, I was already in Brunei. Then I saw my new Boss and their little princess inside their car. I just could not imagine that I was already far from my homeland. I stayed with my boss' sister for a couple of days until we flew to Singapore. While staying there, I met the nanny who could not speak English. The only way to communicate was through hand signs and body language. The foods were all spicy. The clothes were long and there were so

many restrictions that we do not have in the Philippines. There was no traffic and they do not have any public vehicles in their freeways. The country was very peaceful and clean. The culture and traditions were different as expected.

"Respect others the way you want to be respected." *Pranchi*

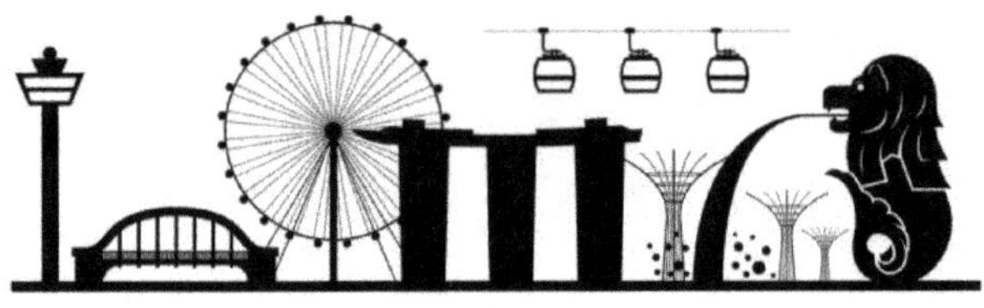

SINGAPORE

PART 9

SINGAPORE TIME

A few days before the Chinese New Year of 2007, we arrived in Singapore. It was a way different scene from Brunei. The country was more developed, there were many tall buildings, unique designs, there was nightlife's and it was a very busy city.

It was my first time to see street dancing and an even more thrilling was seeing was a lion dancing. During those times, I was very busy. Even if there were so many wonderful sights around, I started feeling homesick and I felt alone. The reality starts kicking in me. And there is one more thing, I had to face my battle alone. However, the very thought of turning back never crossed my mind. I needed to be strong. I had nothing to lose. While thinking too much though, it made the time pass by very slowly. And my feeling of loneliness started to become unbearable. I knew I needed to make myself busy to distract myself from being lonely. My goal was to win and survive every day in whatever challenges were at hand. Months, and years passed by and then I started getting used to it. It was probably only a matter of time. My patience was tested. How far could I endure and how strong will I always be. Then I

discovered a solution. I started buying myself small things that make me happy. Each time I went out for a walk, I would visit the library and treated myself to a cup of hot cocoa. Also, I would go to a restaurant and try local food. I finally met new friends named Mary and Grace. Together, we visited nice places around Singapore and my friend Mary shared me encouraging bible verses. Thank God! I won! Working abroad is like winning a lottery. I said so because that was the truth about working abroad for many. Such becomes so if you worked with a boss that shows kindness and generosity. I am proud to say that I think I am among those lucky ones. However, for some, it is an irony. I remembered when my friend Mary told me about this nanny, working with another employer in the same building where she was. Her employer was critical and can be very irritating. She does not get enough rest, not even day-offs, and what is worse was that her boss would not even give her enough food to eat. I met this woman, and we were able to talk. I felt sad and it bothered me that at times I could not even sleep while thinking of her. I tried my best though to help this woman. That is why, before I left Singapore, I asked her if she wanted to come back to the Philippines. I gave her a plane ticket she could use once she decided to go back home. That was the last conversation we had because I had to move back to Brunei with my boss.

“When the righteous cry for help, the Lord hears and rescues them from all their troubles. Isaiah 30:15.”

PART 10

SOCIAL MEDIA

After seven months in Singapore, I finally bought my new phone. Yes, it was a gift for me. Through gadgets and social media, we can communicate with our family, friends, and we could meet different people around the world. Many social media platforms are available. It is important to be very careful on how to use them because there will always be bad users around trying to prey on the innocent.

One day when I came home after sending the kids to their school, I checked my e-mails and there was this website that kept popping up on my computer screen. This was not the first time. I had seen it a couple of times already but I kept ignoring it. This time out of curiosity I clicked just to see what is in it. Heheheh, I was smiling and laughing and admittedly, I was quite excited, because it was a dating site for single people or anyone looking for a partner. Well, I signed up for it. I created my account and I put in one of my ugly pictures for my profile. This website was actually legit. Any of their members could not defraud other members, and if it happened in rare cases, you could report the person and they would immediately take action on your

complaint. Days, weeks, and months passed and by each time I checked my account, I was elated for receiving many messages from different people. Some were nice but some were crazy. During one time, I was checking and browsing some profiles of its members and, OH boy! They were trying to attract anyone by their daring and seductive profile pictures. Yeah, I only looked and I avoid being judgmental of them. I tried reaching out to some of those guys but after a conversation or two, I stopped communicating while I already ignored most of them. However, there was this one sender that caught my attention. He sent me a message, but when I checked his profile picture, it was of two cute little girls and a grandma. Hmmm. I was not so sure if I should send him a reply or not. Well, I chose not to send one. Days passed by and I still had not received any messages from him. I thought it is probably better if I would not reply because I was already thinking that maybe he was not interested or even serious about me. Then one day to my surprise, he sent a message again, so I quickly decided to reply. My first message to him was, "Hello!" followed by introducing myself to him. Then I asked him, "Are you single?" He answered that he is SINGLE. Then I replied, "Are you SURE?" Then, I inquired, "Why does your profile have kids?" He told me, "That is my grandmother and nieces." I believed him that time, but still, I cannot convince myself whether he was telling me the truth. I still doubted him. Social media offers lots of unexpected, crazy, and surprising things. Some could be real many were fake. We have to be careful. We should not easily put our trust in whatever we see that people had posted or written on them.

"Self-care is giving the world the best of you, instead of what's left of you." *Katie Reed*

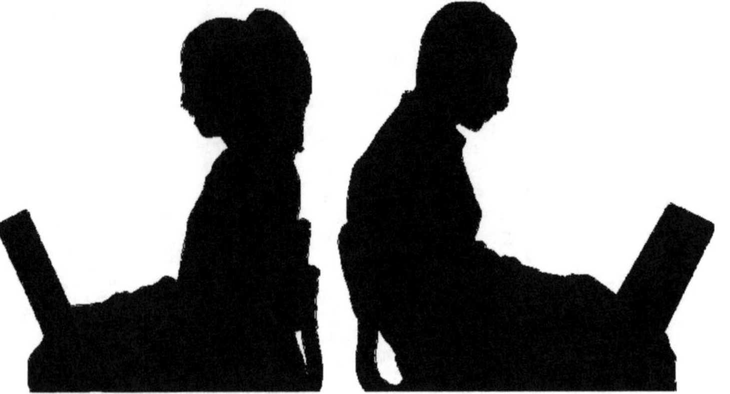

PART 11

CONVERSATION

From the dating website, we moved to communicate through our personal e-mails and phone number. We exchanged our emails and phone numbers. This man was consistently keeping in touch with me. I enjoyed his company and discovered that we had some common things we both wanted. Later on, we became good friends. We talked about our hobbies, jobs and so on. After seven months of exchanging messages, stories, and updates about each other, he wanted to visit me in Singapore. I agreed, so he planned his trip so we could meet. It was so thrilling because he booked his hotel reservation across the street where I lived. Everything was already set but about a month before his trip, I asked him to cancel his flight because of my work. I cannot meet him. My schedule conflicted with his vacation days in Singapore. So, left without a choice, he had to cancel his trip. Our communications with each other kept going regularly. He called me or e-mailed me almost every day. Months went by quickly, until one day when my boss came home from work, he called me and said, "May, I have a new job. It will not be here in Singapore anymore. My job here is done so, we have to go back to Brunei. You have to come with us in Brunei also because your working visa here in Singapore will expire be expiring, too." While I was giving it a thought, a vacation to my country sparked up my mind. I asked my boss if I could get a vacation first before signing in for another work contract with him, and he was okay with it. We flew to Brunei in about two weeks or so and I was not able to communicate with my online friend, not even replying to his messages. Then one time, I asked one of my bosses' drivers if I could use his phone to check on my e-mails. Finally, I was able to read and reply to all of his messages. I told him that I was going back to the Philippines for a short vacation. I asked him if he wanted to meet me in the Philippines instead. He answered back right away saying, "Of course!" Therefore, we were going to meet in the Philippines. I informed him of my arrival date and time in Manila, afterward he booked his plane ticket.

In April 2008, I arrived in Manila my sister picked me up at the airport. I stayed for a couple of weeks in Quezon Province while waiting for him to arrive in the Philippines.

"Everything happens for a reason. Wait on God and trust in him. He wants the best for us. He wants to take us from Glory, and from Victory to Victory." *Germany Kent*

PART 12

OUR FIRST MEETING

In April 2008, my friend and I were ready to meet. I called him my "friend" because we are not yet committed to each other, in other words, there is no "us". Although we were talking every day, we are not yet a couple or lovers. He had not asked me yet if I could become his girlfriend or his special one. We were open-minded, what I meant was I never restricted him from talking to or befriending others and vice versa. Nevertheless, if you asked me whether I liked him or loved him, Yes, I do! The more we talked I started liking him and I developed my feelings toward him over time, but I tried to keep it to myself because I do not want to hope falsely, only to get hurt later.

I established something as a sign during our first meeting. What was the sign that I was thinking of…a KISS! While still giggling over such a thought, I suddenly saw him walking towards me. "OH, NO!" I do not know how to react; I just could not act normally in his presence. Then he came closer then hugged me and kissed me so I kissed him back. I never thought that he was just like me, establishing a sign too! I was laughing when he told me, "My plan was to give you a kiss and if you kissed me back then you are mine." I get

it, had I given him a handshake though, it meant we are just friends. What a co-incident! The thing was, in our conversations the topic about courting never came up. There was not even a shallow memory to recall regarding it. All we ever talked about was our daily activities. It seemed as if we had already known each other for a long time. We even looked for the same sign of a "Simple KISS", and if it happens it means we are destined for each other. On that day, he proposed marriage to me. We were then sitting and just staring at each other. He suddenly asked, "WILL YOU MARRY ME?" I responded, "ARE YOU SURE?" then, "What about you go back to California after your vacation, then think about it further, and then, we could plan to meet again?" He answered, "No. I will marry you first before I go back to California." Wow. I had to come up with a decision on the spot. I answered him based on what I felt for him. As I said, I already had feelings towards him. But I kept it inside because I was still waiting until we meet personally. Now though, the time had come, while he sits before me now proposing marriage. Well, I accepted his proposal. I said YES! Hehehe. Did you know that he proposed to me without a ring? He had his reasons why he did so. He told me, "The reason why I didn't buy you a ring is because I am not sure whether you will say YES or NO." But It was no big deal to me. The important thing was that he was sincere and he loves me.

"You don't meet people by accident. There's always a reason. A lesson or a blessing." *Unknown*

PART 13

OUR FIRST DATE

It was April 2008 and we were officially a couple. On our first date, we went to Tagaytay. We stayed for a couple of days there, visiting some of the tourist Areas. It was fun and I really loved being with him. He enjoyed the local food especially the hotdog on a stick. He is a very simple man, not so hard to please, keeping me at ease, and he was someone you could fall in love with easily. Then we visited his family in Pampanga and Pasig. He met my friends, too. We spent every day together roaming around Manila. Then we went to the US embassy to get the documents needed for our wedding.

He told me that our wedding day must take place as soon as possible because he only had a 3-week vacation. Because of that limited time left, we cannot be together until our papers for the wedding were processed. Then on my 25th birthday, we got married. Wow! It was unbelievable. It was on my list, that I wanted to get married only after I had traveled abroad and at the age of 25. Our wedding was very simple with only my family and close friends as guests. On my father's side, we had grandma, my father's mother, my

two uncles, my father's brothers, and their wives. My aunt, my mother's eldest sister, my eldest half-sister, and my three friends were there, too. My husband's relatives that came were his uncle, the brother of her mother, his father and his cousins, and of course, our godparents. After the ceremony we all went to an 'Eat All You Can' restaurant. We chilled and celebrated our Civil Wedding. It was one of my happiest and most special days ever spent with the ones I loved and cherished. After our wedding day, time seemed to speed up when all I ever wished for was for it to at least slowdown. The only thing I can do every day, therefore, was to cherish and make special memories with my beloved. It is so amazing, that I am now married.

A great relationship doesn't happen because of the love you had in the beginning, but it depends greatly on how you will continue building that love until the end.

PART 14

OUR HONEYMOON

On May 7, 2008, after our Civil wedding, my aunt brought us to Marinduque Island. We stayed for two nights on that island. The place was beautiful, clean, and quiet. I can see the ocean from our place of residence. Every house had fruit trees. The foods were so fresh. My husband enjoyed especially the freshly caught fish. We enjoyed the beach and we loved swimming even though it was raining. We watched street dancing gleefully that day during the celebration of the Moriones Festival. People were dancing in the streets wearing Costumes with colorful headpieces. Then we visited nearby towns. How we loved and enjoyed our simple honeymoon. Thanks to my aunt and our relative who let us stay in their house. I could never forget their warm hospitality.

After two days, we went back to Manila because my husband needed to rebook his flight to California. Then we went back to Pampanga to attend the fiesta of the Black Nazarene. Then the following day we went back to Manila.

Then it was time for him to go back home. It was a sad and emotional moment for both of us. If only there was

a way for me to have a visa speedily, we would go for it. But we had to wait until then.

The flight was early in the morning. His uncle, his aunt, and I sent him to the airport. We didn't say goodbye but instead, we said, “SEE YOU SOON HONEY and I LOVE YOU.” We hugged tight and kissed.

"I just can't wait until you are here in my arms. Kissing my forehead just listening to your voice saying I love you and falling asleep next to you with my head on your chest I just can't wait." *Unknown*

PASSPORT
Ticket
Travel

PART 15

WAITING FOR MY US VISA

I stayed in the Philippines for more than eight months while waiting for my travel documents to be processed. While waiting for my visa, I visited my hometown in Lapaz, Leyte. I traveled by bus because I wanted to get a view of the land, the mountains, and the ocean. It was a twenty-four-hour trip. And I never told anyone that I was coming home. Upon arriving, I saw my grandma lying in bed; she was skinny and could not walk anymore. "Long time no see grandma", I said. She looked at me and was surprised. Huhuhu! She wasn't able to recognize me. So I hugged her and introduce myself clearly to her saying, "Lola this is May", then I saw her face shine and then wore the smile I missed for so long. "Where have you been?" she asked. Then a very long conversation followed. I told her I am already married. She asked where my husband is. I answered, "He left a couple of days ago back in the USA." I wished my husband had a couple of days more to stay in the Philippines so that my grandma could have met him. I touched and held my grandma's hands; I was very happy to see her. She was skinny and could not walk anymore. She touched my skin and said, "Your skin is

very soft and you look beautiful," and smiled. I stayed with her for a couple of days. I gave her baths, cut her nails, and fed her. Then I invited my aunts and uncles for simple meals, so I can catch up with them.

The following day I walked the street toward the house of my teacher, Mrs. Esperanza Pulma, one of my angels, who helped me until I finished high school. I was in front of their house gate knocking but no one answered. I could hear music playing but I could not see anybody inside the house. Then I heard someone's voice from the other side of the street. I turned around and walked towards her. I told her I was looking for Mr. and Mrs. Pulma then the lady answered me, "I'm so sorry they already died years ago." I was silent; I don't know how to react. I was shocked and was very sad to know that they already passed away. The lady then asked, "who are you?" I answered, "Do you not recognize me? I was the kid who always helps Mrs. Pulma with her house chores." I left and walked back home. I was so sad to know that they were gone.

"Wishing you peace to bring comfort, courage to face the days ahead, and loving memories to forever hold in your heart. You are always loved and never forgotten."
Unknown

CALIFORNIA
Eureka
Mt Shasta
Redding
Red Bluff
Chico
Oroville
Cascade Mtns
Coastal Mtns
Mendocino
UCDAVIS
Sacramento
Cal
Berkeley
Stockton
San Francisco
Modesto
S
Lake Tahoe
Sierra Nevada
Monterey
Fresno
Mt Whitney
Coastal Mtns
Bakersfield
Pacific Ocean
San Diego
Golden Gate Bridge
HOLLYWOOD
Los Angeles
DEATH VALLEY NATIONAL PARK
Mojave Desert
Barstow
66
SC
Ventura
Ucla
Pasadena
San Bernardino
Los Angeles
Anaheim
Long Beach
Costa Mesa
Palm Springs
Santa Barbara Channel
Channel Islands
UCSD
San Diego
Colorado River

PART 16

MY TRIP TO CALIFORNIA

The eight months of waiting was finally over. In January 2009, around 5 am, the embassy asked me to report for my interview. Then on February 19, 2009, I received approval for my visa. My husband helped me prepare for my flight making sure I had everything I needed for the trip. We were very happy and excited. Soon we will be together.

On February 27, 2009, Philippine time was my flight to California. It was an 18-hour flight. I finally arrived on February 27, 2009, in California time around nighttime. My husband was waiting for me in the arrival area. Hello, California! The cold weather welcomed me too. We drove to his parents" house where we are to stay. Mom and Dad are waiting for me. I had mixed emotions. I was not so sure what they might expect of me but I just had to be myself, 'what you see is what you get. But they were so kind and adorable. We ate dinner and had a short time bonding with them, and then we rested.

The next morning, I think I woke up late. I did have a good slumber. It was already sunny outside and freezing. I got up; I went for a walk in the park. I could

see the mountain topped with thick snow. It was a cold winter year. I spent the cold wintertime readjusting and adapting to my new circumstance. His parents' house stood inside a gated community. Inside the compound were a park and the school was only a few distances from the house. It was quite a neighborhood; I cannot see other people around most of the time. Everyone had his or her own car. I don't see any public vehicles.
I am working on adjusting to the culture, weather, language, etc.

"Time to open up a new chapter in life, and go to explore a larger center." *Lillian Russel*

PART 17

BACK TO SCHOOL

In January 2010, I started my Pharmacy Technician Program and I took extra classes too, such as English, Math, Reading, and Physical Education. I was excited and at the same time nervous because I still cannot fluently speak the English language. Although I could manage a conversation in English, I was still learning and adjusting for most of it. I always sat by the front row in my classroom because I wanted to hear and see clearly what my professors are discussing. I became acquainted with my classmates. They were from different nationalities. Many were using devices to translate a language. That relaxed me, knowing that I do not struggle with the language alone.

Months passed by and I was getting used to it. My language-speaking got better. I was doing great in all my subjects. After the semester year by the fall of 2012, I received my grades. I was surprised to receive my certificate as ranked among the DEAN's Honor List. I was so happy and elated to show the certificate to my husband. My next semester will be different because I had to take my Math through a FASTRACK. That meant not going to the regular classes as usual. Did you know that I really hated math? It was a huge

challenge for me to pass my math subject. For the semester, I had to enroll in two levels of math and then I could proceed with my Pharmacy Calculation Class. I took the earliest class, in that way I could give myself more time to study and finish my assignment. I could still recall that students filled the classroom when the semester started. Every week though, it keeps decreasing, then, later on, some of my classmates were not coming anymore. By the end of the semester, only less than 10 students passed the class and I am one of them. Wow! I congratulated myself saying, "You did it, girl!" Of course, my husband was very proud of me.

Spring of 2013, I received my Certificate; I was already a Certified Pharmacy Technician. After graduating, I did self-study in preparation for my Board Exam. Months after reviewing, I took my Board Exam. I waited for the result for about a week; Thank God, I passed the test. Yes, it called for a celebration. My husband and I went for dinner. Thank you, my beloved husband, for always believing in me. Thank you my Sister In-law Karen for driving me regularly to my clinical training. Thank you, Mom Trudy and Dad Ric, for letting us stay in your house until we can manage on our own and had our very own house. I thank God for having a new Family in California who always supports my husband and me. I am very lucky and blessed to have them.

"Family is not always about blood sometimes it's about who is there to hold your hand and support you when you need them." *Unknown*

people
emailing
possible
contact
position
first
interview
networking
number
major
persons
employees
employers
applying
career
JOB HUNTING
services
hunting
recommended
best
finding
offers
unemployment
employment
effort
jobs
economic
found
occupations
online
interviewer
amounts
prospective
searching
applicant
potential
price
organizations
resume
generally
recruiters
seekers
decision
main
information
work
writing
interviewing
start

PART 18

FINDING A JOB

Finding a job is not easy especially if you lack experience. I just graduated without much experience. I applied for jobs around the city, but oftentimes I get rejected. Nevertheless, I was determined to get a job whether in a pharmacy, office, mall or restaurant, or just any job. All I wanted to do was work. Months then years passed by and finally, I was hired but it was not in the pharmacy field. Macy's Company hired me. My job was called a “signer”, I prepared and display all the prices of the items in the kids' area. The prices needed an update before the store opened. I worked at Macy's for a year while I was still waiting to get a pharmacy job. I was waiting for my time; I know my time to shine will come soon then I will get my dream job.

One day my friend Bhumika, a pharmacist, told me that her company was hiring and that she recommended me. I sent my application and a week later, I got a call from her company. I went for an interview and right away, they hired me. I was very happy that I got my dream job. I received good reviews and recognition every month. I love working in a pharmacy. The station I worked with was very busy. After I was hired, I learned so many tasks in a few months. However, I had to

resign only after six months because I found another job. My new job was that of working inside a hospital. I worked as a pharmacy clerk. Then after a month, they promoted me to be a pharmacy technician.

I am in my sixth year this year. I started working at the Comprehensive Pharmacy in February 2016. The Comprehensive Pharmacy gave me a chance to pursue my dream to help and start up my community event in my hometown. I thank all the sponsors, supporters, friends, family, Aakf PH team co-workers, and everyone who shared their talents.

"I learned to give not because I have much but because I know exactly how it feels to have nothing." *Unknown*

PART 19

DREAM HOUSE AND THE BABY

It has been almost eight years of staying at his family's house and it is time for us to find our own place. I was very much thankful to them for letting us stay until we can save money to build our own. Now we are ready. We both have a stable job and we already saved money for our dream house. We are ready for our first big purchase. After searching, we finally found a place for our future home; it is located in a new community, with perfect distance to my workplace, while it was a couple of miles from my husband's work.

In March 2017, we received approval to purchase the house, after processing and paying for the down payment, we waited for another four months on its' construction.

While we were waiting, I was feeling some strange changes in me. I started having mood swings and I get a little bit of sickness that goes on and off alternately. I suspected that I might be pregnant already that was why I asked my husband to buy me a pregnancy test. We tried the test and a minute later, whoa! My suspicion was true. The test confirmed that I was PREGNANT! We were so happy and excited. It was on my 34th birthday. Then we spread the good news to my

husband's family that I was pregnant. They were as excited as we were.

During my first trimester, it was quite difficult because I had bouts of bad morning sickness and some scents made me sick and feel uneasy. I lost weight because I was choosy with the food, and I always lost the appetite to eat. I never thought that my first 3 months of pregnancy would be this challenging. Nevertheless, after that, my body's normal condition returned. I remained healthy and I was already very much excited to see my baby.

On the third week of July, our house was finished and was ready to be released to us. One week after moving in, I still could not believe the fact that we are already in our very own house. Can you recall one of my dreams on my list and that was to have our own house? I was not sure when will it ever materialize but surprise! It came true! However, not only that it came true, we even received a very special extra blessing, our Baby Boy.

The day of August 1 was going to be my husband's birthday. And for him, our incoming baby boy was the best gift. My husband is a man with simple dreams and enjoyed a simple life. Even on his special day, he never asked for anything. He was always like that and so was his family. You can just imagine how comforting and joyous it is to be with them.

I gave birth on December 28, 2017. It was a difficult delivery. I was in labor for 32 hours and I ended up giving birth via cesarean section. I thanked God that we

got through safe. When I woke up inside the delivery room, the nurse quickly moved me to the recovery room. Then after a couple of minutes or an hour of sleep after the surgery, I first saw my baby and he made me cry for joy. My husband was there, he never left my side and kept waiting for me. The nurse handed me my baby placing him on my chest. Wow! A beautiful and perfect gift and it was fulfilling. Congratulations, we are parents now.

"Expect the unexpected, because God might surprise you with something that you've always wanted even if you didn't expect it to come around so soon." *Unknown*

PART 20

NOW AND FOREVER

Life is so beautiful and unpredictable. We are determined to continue our journey and adventures, but this time it will have to be with our son. We wanted to enjoy life with him while he is still young. We have the goal of living a simple life and continue growing. To keep enjoying life to the fullest always becomes a blessing to others. I will never stop praying to God to guide us in all the things we do. I am still in the process of reaching my long-term goal. I know it will still take time. I am expecting that we might encounter interesting obstacles along the way. However, I am not in a hurry, I will take one step at a time. My families are always with me, they are my strength. The time will come when, God only knows, my goals will come true.

I would like to take this opportunity to thank everyone. I am very blessed to meet different people from my different workplaces and from where I traveled. Thank you for believing in me, especially my community works in the Philippines. Let us continue our journey with more adventures.

"The road ahead may be long but you'll make it there safe and sound."

DEDICATION TO MY GRANDPARENTS

I wrote this book as a dedication for my Grandma Felicidad, and Grandpa Elias. I know you are with me all the way, wherever I go. You are my Guardian Angel who always guided and protected me every day. Thank you for taking good care of me, and my siblings. I wish you had seen those wonderful blessings I was enjoying while you were still alive. Back then, I was still searching and working hard to get a better life. I was still in school finishing my courses. I was not where I am right now. I will do my best to help your son and daughter, especially the person who took care of you when you were sick and who never left until your last breath. I am sending you my hug wherever you are. I love you.

MESSAGE TO MY HUSBAND

My love, you know how much I love you. We have been thru ups and downs. You were always there pushing me behind, supporting, inspiring, guiding, and helping me to achieve my goals and dreams. I never forgot what you asked me when I arrived in California in February 2009, it was, "What would you like to do?" My answer was, "I want to go back to school. I want to study and interact more with people." You answered me, "yes, okay but first, you have to learn how to drive a car because if you don't know how to drive a car you cannot go anywhere." You were my first teacher in speaking the language, in driving a car and so on. You helped me plan everything one-step at a time. During our visit to the Chaffey College School to inquire what courses are available to start up with, you saw how excited I was looking up the classes available in the brochure until the Pharmacy Technician Class caught and nailed my attention. At that very moment, I told you, I wanted to take that Class right away. You were by my side when I went to the Dean's office to inquire about the requirements and the preparations needed like the school transcript to be able to take the course. That same year you enrolled me in a driving class and the school program.

You have seen how far I've grown and achieved my dreams. I am aware of how proud you are of me.

I love you.

Your Wife

MESSAGE TO MY SON

My son, you are the precious gift I received from God. I am so happy to see you every day. Your first step made our hearts leap for joy and the first word you uttered brought us so much joy as they were like music to our ears. I can't wait until you grow up and read your mother's first book. I waited 10 years to have you. This book is like a time machine that will send you back through the time of your mother's journey. You will soon understand and discern why your mother teaches you at a young age to be kind and to show respect to others. I may have much to give materially, but we, your father and I promise that we will provide you with your education and will lovingly guide and support you in the many decisions you will be making in time. We will not expect anything in return but we want you to do whatever you desire as long as it won't hurt you.
I love you.

Mommy

MESSAGE TO MS. REYCHEL MAWAC

Girl, thank you for sharing your good vibe and writing resources so I could continue to write my story. This way I can keep supporting all my Community Activities. I feel that you are my Soul mate and Angel that can always read my mind even though we are a million miles away.

Sending Love

Mayvel

MESSAGE TO AAKF PH TEAM

Each one of you has a unique talent. The moment you stood on your feet to the ground and walked toward the events, you already started creating a memory for yourself, your team/family, and especially to the children and the whole community. Thank you for always creating beautiful activities for the children and making the entire Barangay SMILE. We are millions of miles apart but it seems like all of you are standing right next to me and we are walking side by side in all our activities. Thank you for sharing your talents with AAKF PH.

Sending Love.

Mayvel

MESSAGE TO ROLLAND ORONOS

Kuya Rolland, thank you so much for sharing your talent with All About Kids Foundation PH. I am very happy and proud of you for creating my book cover too. Please continue to share your talent not only for me but for others too. God bless you
Sending Love

Mayvel

MESSAGE TO ALL THE READERS

Every day we encounter different scenes in life. Sometimes we experience dark days sometimes we enjoy bright days. Embracing both will make us strong and will help keep us moving forward. Let us embrace and enjoy life because we only live one time. Smile more and share it with the world.

Thank you for spending time reading my book.
Spread Kindness.

Mayvel

REVIEW FROM THE READERS

Congratulations on your first book my sister. I am so proud of your strength and courage to write your book "Journey with Unexpected Proposal" and to share your story with the world. I know that everyone who will read your stories will be inspired. I am so happy and proud of you sister. I love you.

Sister,
ZharinaBorela

To my auntie and my godmother: Congratulations on your new book. I cannot wait to read it. I know it will be a very beautiful story that everyone should read. Thank you for inspiring my siblings and me always. Thank you also for always reminding us to focus on our education. I wish you all the best.

Love,
Zhyra May Borela

Ms. Mayvel, congratulations on your new book the "Journey with Unexpected Proposal". Thank you for letting me read your manuscript before it gets published. I am amazed by your courage that no matter how tough life becomes you never gave up. Instead, you keep on striving for your goals and kept reminding yourself that it is better to be ambitious and be the best person you can be always.

Love,
Kitel Abordo
Student /Aakf PH Volunteer

The "Journey with Unexpected Proposal" is a book that gives inspiration to all ages. Thru faith and determination, everything is possible. Your story is one of the living examples that everyone can apply in their life. Your willingness, kindness, and faith in God helped you to keep moving forward and continue in your journey. Your selfless determination to help children in the Philippines is a Gem. If the young generations will have the same mindset as yours, it is possible for all of their dreams to come true.

Reychel L. Mawac
Author (Batang Ina)

The "Journey with Unexpected Proposal" is a truly amazing and inspiring book. The author shared and gave us beautiful lessons in life. She showed that poverty and obstacles in life are not hindrances to reaching our dreams in life. The author of this book reminded us that everything happens for a reason, just believe in yourself, be positive in life always, and have faith in God.

Janice Mauro
Educator /Aakf PH Coordinator

The "Journey of Unexpected Proposal" is a heart-melting story of the author herself. From her childhood days up to her married life. She shared and toured us through her various emotions of happiness, sadness, excitements, struggles, longings, faith, determination, and courage. She is a genuine and brave writer who shared her true-to-life journey to readers of all ages without hesitations. A must-read book!

Bernadith De La Cruz
Author of "A Call to Remember- A Journey with the Swiss" book.

The "Journey with Unexpected Proposal" is a story igniting connections with everyone, yes, everyone in our country, the Philippines. Anyone reading her story can relate and probably connect. Your determination, courage, positivity, and hard work are something that I hoped everyone had. Good luck and God bless you, sis, you deserved all the best that happened in your life including your dream that came true, besides having a loving family around you. Keep it up and continue touching the lives of many.

Lina Garceniego
Accountant

Sister, congratulations on your new book the "Journey with Unexpected Proposal", a very inspiring story of courage and the power of determination. kudos sis! I want to thank you for being such a nice friend and a blessing to everyone!

Aj Serrano
Friend

Mayvel congratulation on your first book. I feel you did a great job putting it together. It helped me see the struggle you lived through and I love the quotes you say at the end of each paragraph.

David Delgadillo
Certified Pharmacy Technician

Mayvel congratulation on your first book "Journey with Unexpected Proposal," I love how you broke it down in sections. I wish you nothing but the best. I hope you much success. Love you. Best wishes!

Janon Jordan
Certified Pharmacy Technician

ABOUT THE AUTHOR

Mayvel B. Datuin is a Filipino immigrant, a woman with ambition and with a heart of gold. Currently living in California "The Golden State", married for 13 years and a mother. The Founder of All About Kids Foundation PH (AAKF PH), a non-profit organization actively running since 2016. She is a Certified Pharmacy Technician for nine years.

"You will face many defeats in life, but never let your self be defeated." *Maya Angelou*

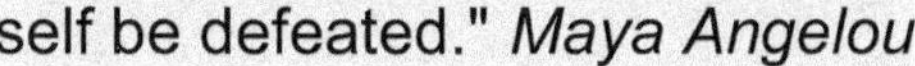

www.ingramcontent.com/pod-product-compliance
Lightning Source LLC
LaVergne TN
LVHW010117170826
845678LV00012B/2462

* 9 7 8 6 2 1 4 7 0 1 8 6 5 *